NEW HOTELS 3

NEW HOTELS 3

Àgata Losantos

COLLINS|DESIGN

An Imprint of HarperCollins*Publishers*

NEW HOTELS 3
Copyright © 2006 by COLLINS DESIGN and LOFT Publications

First edition published in 2005 by:
Loft Publications
Via Laietana 32 4.º of. 104
08003 Barcelona. Spain
Tel.: +34 932 688 088
Fax: +34 932 680 425
www.loftpublications.com

English language edition first published in 2006 by:
Collins Design
An Imprint of HarperCollins*Publishers*
10 East 53rd Street
New York, NY 10022
Tel.: (212) 207-7000
Fax: (212) 207-7654
collinsdesign@harpercollins.com
www.harpercollins.com

Distributed throughout the world by:
HarperCollins*Publishers*
10 East 53rd Street
New York, NY 10022
Fax: (212) 207-7654

Editor: Àgata Losantos
Research: Marta Casado
Art director: Mireia Casanovas Soley
Translation: Jane Wintle
Layout: Oriol Serra Juncosa

Library of Congress Cataloging-in-Publication Data

Losantos, Àgata.
  New hotels 3 / Àgata Losantos.—1st ed.
    p. cm.
  ISBN-13: 978-0-06-089343-9 (hardcover)
  ISBN-10: 0-06-089343-5 (hardcover)
  1. Hotels. 2. Hotels—Decoration. 3. Interior architecture—History—20th
century. 4. Interior architecture—History—21st century. I. Title: New hotels
three. II. Title.

  NA7800.N493 2006
  910.46'09'0511—dc22

                    2005034966

Printed by: I.Graficas Marmol S.L
Spain
DL: B-14.806-06
First Printing, 2006

CONTENTS

8 INTRODUCTION

10 URBAN OASIS

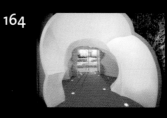

INTRODUCTION

Choosing a hotel can be one of the most difficult tasks we face when we are planning a trip. The limitations of time and money, the availability of rooms, and the need to stay at one particular place on the planet and not another all significantly affect our final decision. Imagine that just one time we could choose a hotel that most closely suited our personality and travel style. Which hotel would we stay at?

For their creators, hotels present an opportunity to imagine a setting that is not a home—and should not resemble one, either, but rather surpass one. Guests do not simply stay at the hotel but live there, if for only one night. Consequently, it should leave an impression. In a world where distances are shrinking and prices falling, it is becoming harder to achieve this. How does one impress the visitor who has already set foot in the major cities of the five inhabited continents of the world?

Architecturally speaking, a hotel also presents the opportunity to challenge the esthetic uniformity that currently plagues the design of public places. The search for a misunderstood modernity has spawned a generation of dismal clones all over the planet, in no way lightening the dreary burden of endless preconceived ideas afflicting the traditional hotel industry.

Hotels now contain cultural centers as well as 24-hour bars, offer personal assistants rather than receptionists, and feature various types of cuisine. Hoteliers have quickly recognized that ongoing changes in taste and needs within society call for a "live or die" approach to hotel service as a priority objective. The concept of "luxury" is continually evolving: It no longer means providing ostentatious spaces, full of glitz and chandeliers. Today's visitors want to feel unique simply because of where they are staying, which means that, nowadays, luxury is a matter of finding that sought-after "special" difference. In light of this, the hotels featured in this book constitute the ultimate expression of this conception of luxury. Each one has its own personality born of a union between innovation and local character. Without the former, there is no progress; without the latter, hotels run the risk of fading into that great morass of inconspicuous modern absurdity.

URBAN OASIS

All large cities on our planet offer a great variety of hotels that cater to a very diverse public. Behind façades that reflect local architecture, the uniqueness of the hotels described here is found in their interior design and the attentive service that ensures the comfort of guests. On crossing the hotel threshold, guests discover a different world, where the bustle of the city can be temporarily forgotten but not completely abandoned: a perfect balance of calm and activity that beckons like a personal oasis, a place of refuge in the midst of the anonymity of the large metropolis.

HOTEL CRAM

The Eixample quarter of Barcelona, which was built up primarily between the nineteenth and twentieth centuries, encompasses beautiful examples of modernist architecture. The two side-by-side buildings described here were originally erected in 1892. GCA Arquitectes Associats, with extensive experience in hotels, undertook the complete conversion of these buildings into the Hotel Cram. The project involved gutting the buildings, preserving only the façades.

The stately hotel exterior contrasts strikingly with its modern interior. The main corridors circle around a central toplit atrium, which houses the large vertical spaces containing the elevators. The light entering from above establishes a link between the private and public spaces inside.

The plan consists of three floors below ground level and seven above. The first basement holds several multiple-use halls, and the other two underground floors are dedicated to parking space. The double-height ground floor, where black tones on the floors and ceilings offer a pleasing contrast to the subtle shades of red on the furniture and curtains, is occupied by a reception area, the lobby, and the renowned Gaig restaurant on the mezzanine floor. Extensive windows dramatically situate the hotel lobby in the midst of the milling activity outside, while shielding the interior from the busy traffic. The rooms on the six floors above are equipped with a range of lighting plans that enable different effects to be created in each room to suit each guest's individual mood.

One of the most outstanding features of this project is the counterpoint of light and dark spaces, which is a recurrent theme throughout the hotel. This device allows different environments, each with its own unique characteristics, to be linked and enhanced through a carefully chosen combination of materials.

Architects: **Josep Riu/GCA Arquitectes Associats**
Collaborators: **Beatriz Cosials, Francisco de Paz**
Photography: **Jordi Miralles**
Opening date: **2004**
Number of rooms: **67**
Address: **Aribau 54, Barcelona, Spain**
Telephone: **+34 932 167 700**
Fax: **+34 932 167 707**
E-mail: **info@hotelcram.com**
Web site: **www.hotelcram.com**
Services: **bars, restaurant, conference rooms, swimming pool**

Light chases dark throughout the hotel. On all the floors dedicated to guest rooms, overhead light from the central atrium dissolves in the shadows of the corridors which, in turn, give way to the bright bedrooms, designed in very pale tones.

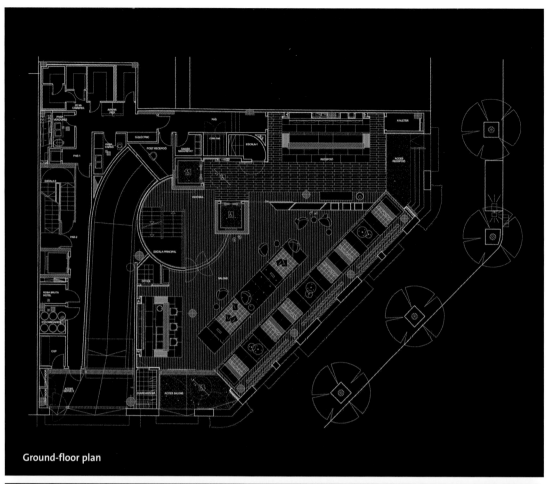

Ground-floor plan

Type plan

CONDESAdf

During the first quarter of the twentieth century, the art nouveau movement and orderly town planning molded the Condesa district, which today is a sanctuary for a fertile amalgamation of up-and-coming businesses and bohemian artists. CONDESAdf, named in honor of the district in which it is located, occupies an original building from 1928 that sits at an intersection of sheltered streets near Parque España.

The architectural project consisted of building an open courtyard reminiscent of a Mexican hacienda, whose form reproduces the triangular plan of the building. The courtyard visually unifies all the public spaces within the hotel, suggesting numerous interpretations and applications. On all floors a wrap-around balcony, protected by shutters, opens onto this open space, which is the heart of CONDESAdf. Among the remaining common areas are the terrace, noteworthy for its sushi bar, which offers splendid views across the adjacent streets and park, and the basement, where the disco is found.

India Mahdavi selected "new chic" as an interior design style, which brings an informal and relaxed attitude to modern forms. The furnishings, also selected by the interior designer, draw on 1950s and '60s styles and fine-tune the simple charm that the entire hotel epitomizes. The individual rooms were conceived to convey a peaceful feel, in this city characterized by constant bustle. The local design influence is evident in the extensive use of artisanal wood and carpeting from the Oaxaca region. Every room has a balcony or terrace and, the warm retro experience notwithstanding, is fitted with the latest technological innovations.

Initiated by the same promoters as the Deseo and Habita hotels, whose contemporary design has made them into noteworthy points of reference in Mexico, CONDESAdf has not followed the same minimalist formula of those earlier successes. Instead, one finds a hotel that celebrates the rich social and cultural traditions of the district.

Architects: **Javier Sánchez/Higuera + Sánchez**
Designer: **India Mahdavi**
Photography: **Undine Pröhl**
Opening date: **2005**
Number of rooms: **40**
Address: **Avenida Veracruz 102, Colonia Condesa, Mexico DF, Mexico**
Telephone: **+52 55 5241 2600**
Fax: **152 55 5241 2640**
E-mail: **info@condesadf.com**
Web site: **www.condesadf.com**
Services: **bar, restaurant, dance club, shop, roof terrace, energy room, Turkish bath**

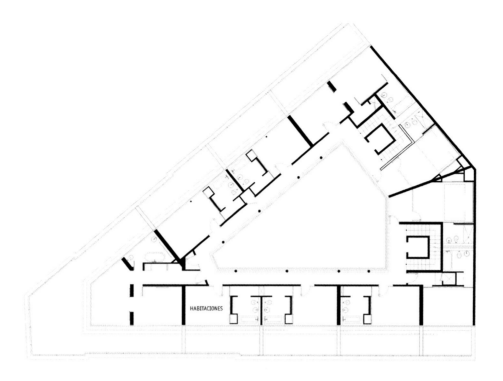

Ground-floor plan

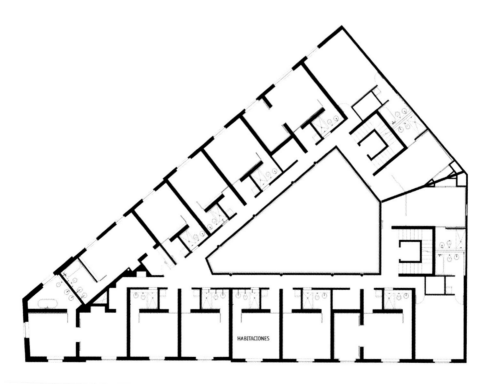

Type plan

Designer India Mahdavi reinterpreted Mexican modernism, merged it with local tradition, and added a European touch to create these 40 unique hotel rooms and suites.

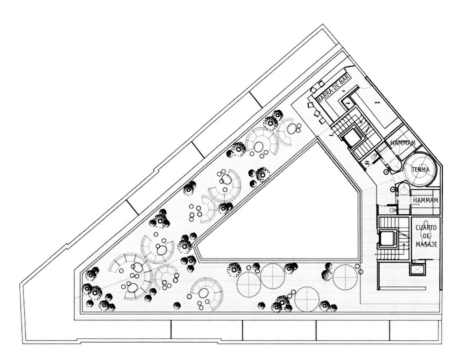

Roof-floor plan

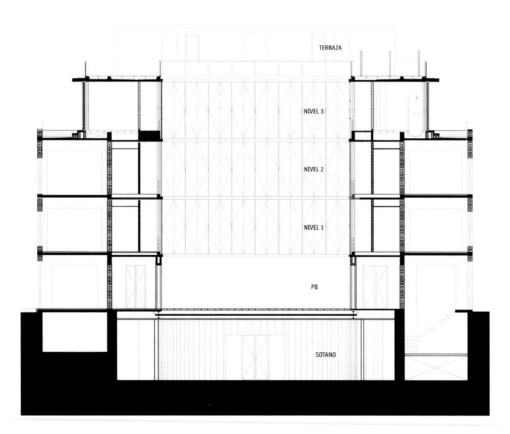

Section

HÔTEL LE A

Hôtel Le A lies within the Triangle d'Or, one of Paris's most distinguished and exclusive districts, a stone's throw from the Champs Élysées. The combined work of designer Frédéric Méchiche and artist Fabrice Hybert, where rooms are adjacent to the spacious lounge/bar, this hotel evokes the feeling of being inside the home of an art collector rather than a traditional hotel.

The ground-floor lobby, flooded with natural light entering through the glass roof, gives way to a separate reception area, an impressive library with a large collection of books on art and design, and the elegant bar with a black-and-white décor. The shortage of space led Méchiche to avoid installing doors and corridors as much as possible, reducing partitions to the minimum. Hybert placed two pieces of his artwork in this area, to complement the dark wood tones, white walls, and heavy chocolate-colored velvet drapes. The carefully devised lighting scheme, with a hanging fixture repeated in every room, is one of the project's most prominent features. The elevator, next to a fresco by Hybert, is a white cubicle that takes on the color of each different floor it travels past. A palette of white walls, dark wood paneling, and chrome highlights is common to all 25 rooms, each of which is distinguished by original artwork by Hybert and personalized with a different theme. The door to each room features a brief description of the artwork within, for the benefit of guests.

The theme of all the paintings, frescoes, and tapestries created by Hybert for Méchiche revolves around the interactions among hotel, city, and guests—the city as a maze waiting for guests, the hotel's anonymous temporary residents.

Designer: **Frédéric Méchiche**
Photography: **Hôtel Le A**
Opening date: **2003**
Number of rooms: **25**
Address: **4 rue d'Artois, Paris, France**
Telephone: **+33 1 42 56 99 99**
Fax: **+33 1 42 56 99 90**
E-mail: **info@hotel-le-a.com**
Web site: **www.paris-hotel-a.com**
Services: **bar, library**

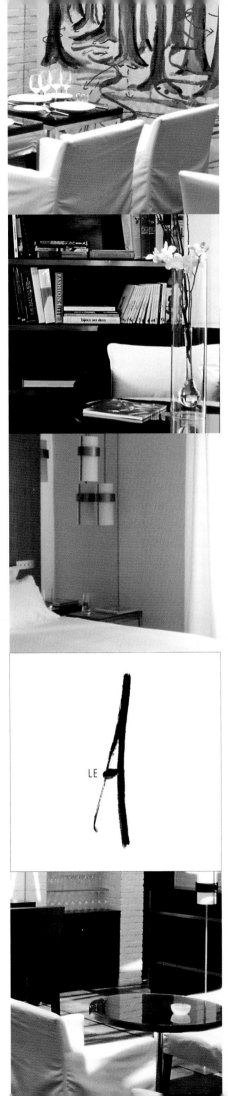

Modern influences in Hybert's work are the only jarring notes in the classi-
cal, harmonious design of these rooms, heightening their prominence.

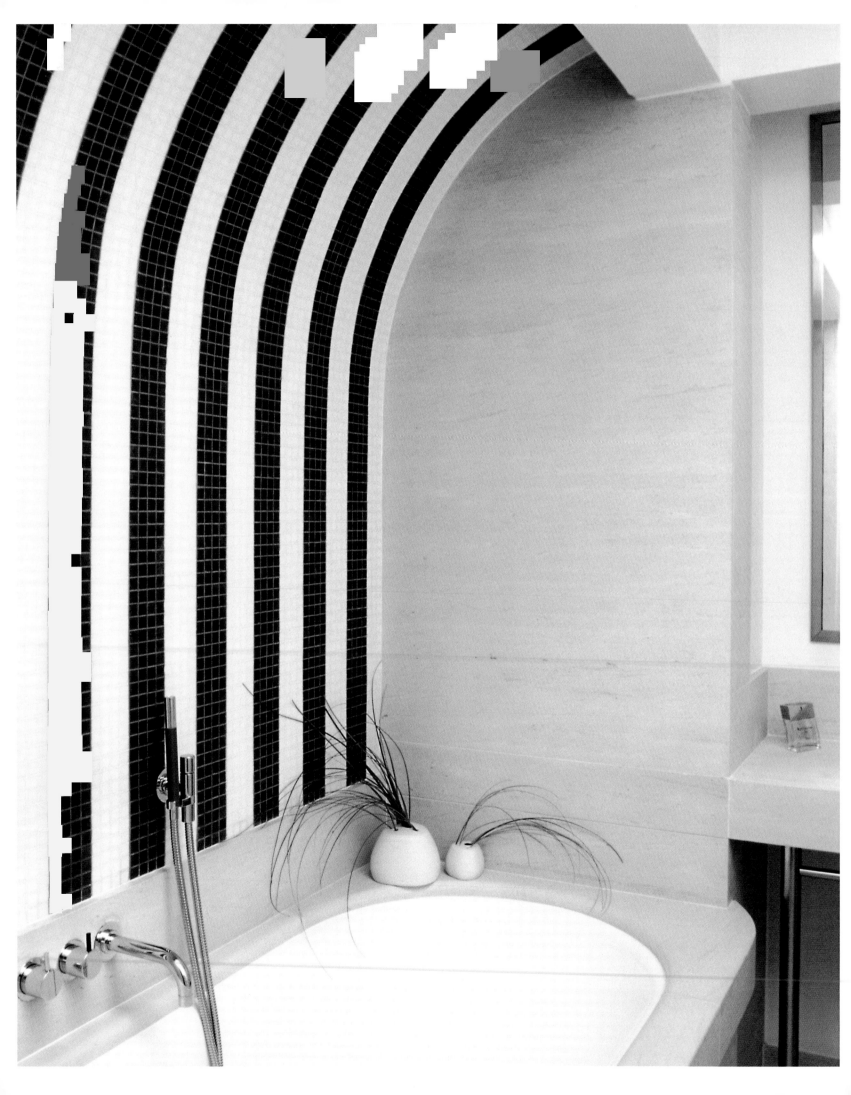

casa camper
barcelona

CASA CAMPER

Camper, the famous shoe brand created in Majorca in 1975, has embarked upon a new venture with Casa Camper, a hotel following the same principles of "comfort and imagination." Located in the busy multicultural Raval neighborhood, the hotel occupies a nineteenth-century structure that has been completely rebuilt except for the pre-neoclassical façade.

Founder Lorenzo Fluxà, a seasoned hotelier, wanted to offer guests precisely what he found lacking when traveling. The entrance hallway appears intentionally confusing and combines a variety of styles and functions: a luxurious black marble counter on a wooden support, showcases with products for sale, a large Hannah Collins mural, and several virtual maps of the city. At the back of the hallway is the bar, inspired by airport VIP lounges, where a pick-me-up snack may be enjoyed at any hour of the day.

The elevators, which, like the rest of the building, boast work by the distinguished designer América Sánchez, descend to conference rooms in the basement or ascend to four floors of orderly accommodations. On entering the corridor at any of the four levels, visitors are guided by a two-color coded system consisting of red for sleeping quarters and white for daytime areas. Casa Camper offers two separate areas instead of the traditional suite—one for work or relaxation, which overlooks the street, and another for sleeping, overlooking the tranquility of the interior aspidistra garden. Furniture and fixtures were carefully chosen based on the informed experience of project director Fernando Amat, who is also the driving force behind the popular Vinçon store, where classic design coexists with the latest fashion trends. The top floor, in addition to housing the service areas and installations, also boasts a flat-roof terrace from which magnificent views of the city may be enjoyed.

casa camper
barcelona

Architects: **Fernando Amat/Vinçon, Jordi Tió**
Photography: **Sandro Garofalo**
Opening date: **2005**
Number of rooms: **25**
Address: **Elisabets 11, Barcelona, Spain**
Telephone: **+34 933 426 280**
Fax: **+34 933 427 563**
E-mail: **casabcn@camper.com**
Web site: **www.casacamper.com**
Services: **bar with free snacks served all day, conference rooms, outdoor terrace, vertical garden, wireless Internet access in rooms, bike rental**

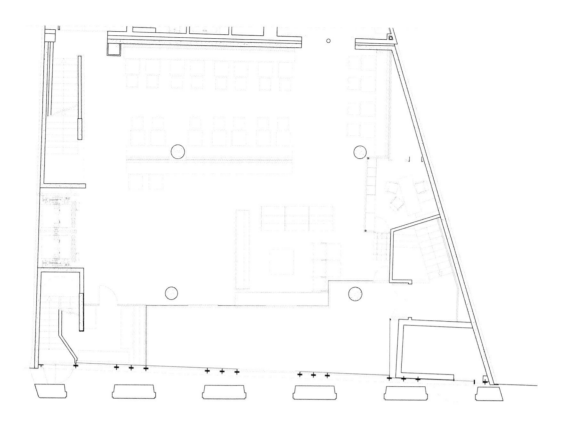

Ground-floor plan

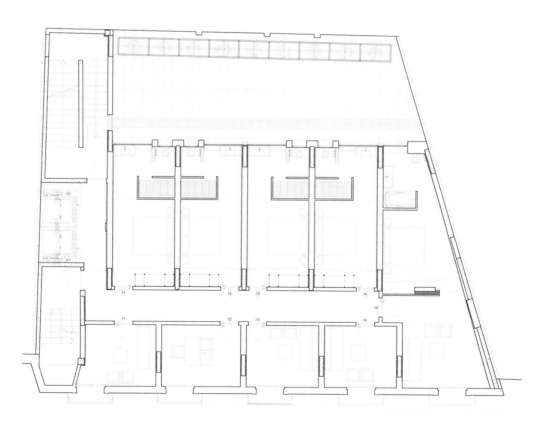

Type plan

Guests at Casa Camper will be pleasantly surprised to discover details they may have found lacking in their experience of other hotels. These include a bar that is open round the clock, a coatrack running the whole length of the room, and city maps readily available in both the private and the common areas of the hotel premises.

MURANO URBAN RESORT

Located to the north of the Marais district, Murano Urban Resort combines classicism with modernity behind an original nineteenth-century façade. After more than two years' continuous work, designers Christine Derory and Raymond Morel created a new concept in contemporary comfort in which luxury and technology take leading roles.

The entrance to the hotel opens into a white marble gallery lined with glass sculptures that reflect the interior light coming from the glass ceiling. The lobby features a beautiful 20-foot fireplace built into the main wall, with a tempting white leather chesterfield sofa opposite, inviting guests to unwind from the bustle of the city.

The 52 white rooms, each with an Italianate name, are brought to life with colorful lithographic prints in pure Roy Lichtenstein style as well as contemporary furniture and works of art, lending a fashionable touch to the otherwise immaculate space. An ingenious system of lighting permits guests to choose according to their mood.

The bar presents two aspects: by day, natural light pervades the room through large windows, which at night are covered to create an intimate and warm atmosphere, enhanced by red carpets and upholstered walls. The ingenious combination of baroque and contemporary design that characterizes the restaurant is topped by a graceful forest of stalactites suspended from the 16-foot-high ceiling.

Starting from the premise of creating a humanistic establishment within a contemporary esthetic, the designers came up with these simple forms, quality materials, and stunning color contrasts. In addition to furnishings from leading design firms of recent decades, numerous artists participated in the project; among these, the legendary Murano glasswork is outstanding.

Designers: **Christine Derory, Raymond Morel**
Photography: **Grégoire Gardette**
Opening date: **2005**
Number of rooms: **52**
Address: **13 boulevard du Temple, Paris, France**
Telephone: **+33 1 42 71 20 00**
Fax: **+33 1 42 71 21 01**
E-mail: **paris@muranoresort.com**
Web site: **www.muranoresort.com**
Services: **bar, restaurant, spa, gym**

Pop Art themes appear against the monochromatic white rooms, illuminated
in such a way that the atmosphere may be tuned to suit guests' moods.

THE SCARLET

Situated within one of Singapore's historic districts and close to the business center of the city, The Scarlet occupies a row of original houses from 1868 as well as a 1924 art deco building, all refurbished to present a boldly luxurious and opulent combination.

Remaining faithful to the district's predominant architectural style, the interior designers conceived an esthetic wherein splendor derives from the noble quality of the materials and the warm, almost fiery color combinations. Scarlet, the hotel's namesake, is the main protagonist, along with sumptuous gold and the sophisticated blacks of the mahogany and lacquers.

On stepping through the main entrance, guests see two golden mosaic fountains that flank the path to the impressive reception desk, fashioned from a solid piece of black marble with white veins. The sheer opulence of the entrance hall, which is enhanced by shimmering reflections from the Venetian glass chandelier off the black flooring and numerous mirrors, previews the style that guests will experience throughout the rest of the hotel.

Five of the 84 rooms are thematically designed suites, each suggestively named: the purple, aubergine, and violet Splendour Palace; the Passion suite featuring pomegranates and fuchsias; the Opulent suite, where green dominates the walls and floors; the olive green Lavish suite; and the Swank suite, with coordinated bright silver walls, curtains, and furniture. As in these five suites, the remaining rooms contain an abundance of mahogany, cornucopia mirrors, and marble baths.

The combination of reds, blacks, and gold is carried out within the conference room and the main restaurant, while the Breeze open-air restaurant on the roof terrace offers a subtler alternative, exhibiting muted tones of teak flooring with a canopied roof.

Architects: **Hia HK**
Photography: **The Scarlet**
Opening date: **2004**
Number of rooms: **84**
Address: **33 Erskine Road, Singapore**
Telephone: **+65 6511 3333**
Fax: **+65 6511 3303**
E-mail: **enquiry@thescarlethotel.com**
Web site: **www.thescarlethotel.com**
Services: **bars, restaurants, conference room, gym, roof terrace**

The rooftop restaurant offers a fine panoramic view over the tiled roofs surrounding the hotel and of the distant skyscrapers in the financial district.

The Passion room was designed specially for honeymooning newlyweds.
Low ceilings create an intimate setting, while the Jacuzzi on the terrace
provides the ideal place to relax and enjoy the magnificent vistas of the city.

HOTEL SEZZ

Located within the elegant Passy residential district, and far removed from the tourist trail, Hotel Sezz occupies one of Paris's characteristic stone-façade buildings, with numerous symmetrical openings and forged iron ornaments. The neo-classic environment heightens the impact of the innovative interior design by Christophe Pillet, a former student of Philippe Starck.

The entranceway to the Sezz does not contain a reception desk; this function has been replaced by a personal assistant for each guest. Two rooms flank the entranceway, designed in red and brown hues, which contrast with the gray Cascais stone that is abundant throughout the building. The bar is located on the ground floor, while the Turkish bath, the Jacuzzi, and the massage salon can be found in the basement.

The 27 rooms are distributed on the seven remaining floors. Throughout, the somber tones of the gray Cascais stone and the dark parquet flooring are enhanced by the contrasting intense colors of the carpets and sofas. The most well-known contemporary design firms, including Christophe Pillet himself, are represented in the hotel's furniture and accessories. The bed is centrally located within each room, and the bathroom is integrated into the bedroom, separated only by a glass screen. For the hotel's sponsors, twenty-first-century luxury has more to do with spaciousness and service than with extravagant details. For this reason, bedroom sizes vary between 60 and 120 square feet enhanced visually by the minimalist style and absence of partitioning.

Designer: **Christophe Pillet**
Photography: **Manuel Zublena**
Opening date: **2005**
Number of rooms: **27**
Address: **6 avenue Frémiet, Paris, France**
Telephone: **+33 1 56 75 26 26**
Fax: **+33 1 56 75 26 16**
E-mail: **mail@hotelsezz.com**
Web site: **www.hotelsezz.com**
Services: **bar, conference room, Jacuzzi, Turkish bath, massage room**

Cool, dark stone on the walls and floors is counterbalanced by the delicate play of light and dashes of intense, vivid color.

HOTEL BÁSICO

Over the last few decades Playa del Carmen, about 37 miles south of Cancún, has become an important tourist center on Mexico's Caribbean coast. Hotel Básico stands out among the hundreds of other hotels along the shoreline, evoking an essential impression of the authentic Mexican spirit, unpretentiously combining a good measure of originality with contemporary design. The intent of architects Isón and Sánchez was to recreate typical Mexican civic architecture as seen in schools, public markets, and bathing resorts, with clear references to local trades, such as blacksmith's forges, fruit stalls, fishmongers, and gasoline stations, employed for contrast.

Hotel Básico is only a few yards from the sea, next to the busy 5th Avenida. The Caribbean sand mixed into the cement makes the building glisten in the sun. The ground floor houses the basic hotel functions and service areas with three additional floors and the roof terrace above. The hotel lobby is a long space—roughly, 50 feet—which creates the impression of a market open to the street, without doors or walls. The walls throughout the building have been left as bare concrete, while the flooring is made from recycled wood. The reception area, which also doubles as a juice bar, transforms itself into a lively lounge at night. At the rear of the lobby is the elevator—actually more like a hoist—around which a stairway ascends.

The rooms on the next two stories are arranged around a central courtyard on the first floor, where an enormous tree grows, rising high above the roof. This open space also contains the restaurant, designed to resemble market stalls, and the completely open kitchen. In the rooms, the cement walls and visible fixtures create an almost industrial feeling. Recycled materials and references to diverse trades are once again found on the roof terrace, where two ancient, red-colored cisterns have been converted into glamorous swimming pools with breathtaking views of the Caribbean Sea.

Architects: **Moisés Isón, José Antonio Sánchez/Central de Arquitectura**
Designer: **Héctor Galván/Omelette**
Photography: **Undine Pröhl**
Opening date: **2005**
Number of rooms: **15**
Address: **5ª Avenida y Calle 10 Norte, Playa del Carmen, Quintana Roo, Mexico**
Telephone: **+52 984 879 44 48**
Fax: **+52 984 879 44 49**
Web site: **www.hotelbasico.com**
Services: **bars, restaurant, roof terrace, swimming pool**

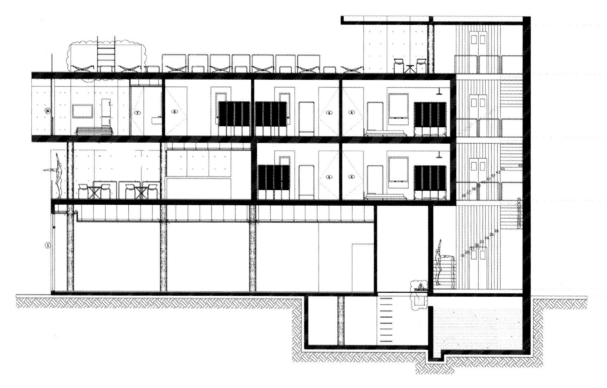

Section

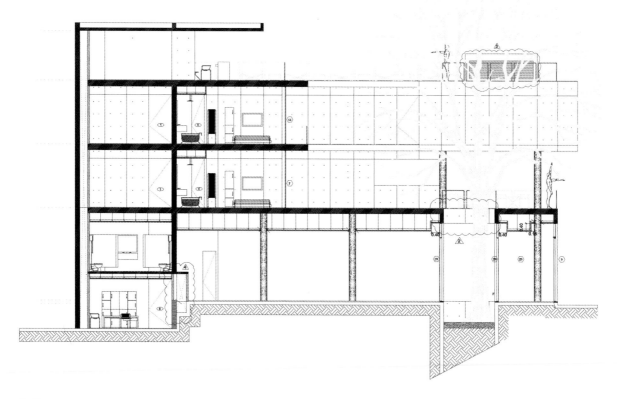

Section

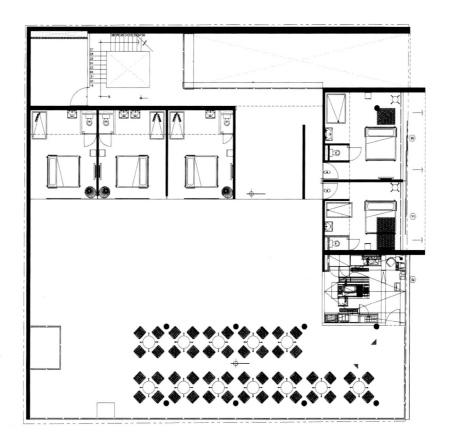

First-floor plan

Second-floor plan

The deep red color of the old water tanks, converted into swimming pools on the rooftop, is a reminder of an industrial past.

Access to guest rooms is gained from a balcony running the length of the building, overlooking the interior patio, where the restaurant is located.

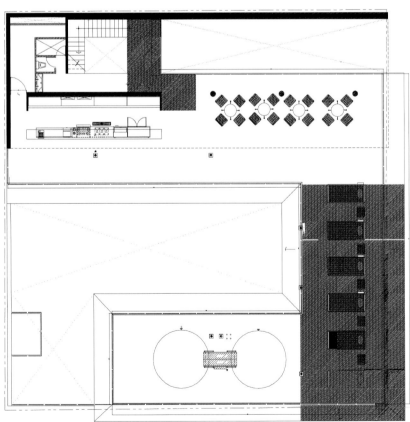

Roof-floor plan

FRESH HOTEL

The Fresh Hotel is located in multicultural, multicolored Athens city center. Built on the foundations of an earlier, more pedestrian hotel that opened in 1976, the Fresh Hotel was designed to hold a double dialogue with its surroundings. On one hand, the building reflects the hustle and bustle in the neighborhood, with the brilliant colors and play of light on the façade, and on the other hand, thanks to the use of modern materials and architectural techniques, it epitomizes the future of this quarter where massive renovation is already in full swing.

Guests access the hotel through a double-height hall, where the remarkable furniture and lighting scheme are the work of premier names in contemporary design. On the left, a long, low fireplace runs along a dramatic black wall. To the right, the reception area is framed by translucent acid pink glazing that matches the color of the counter. Beyond, the white flagstones in the lobby give way to walnut flooring and wall paneling in the bar, where a long orange Corian counter suggests the source of the hotel's name. The expanse of the walls is broken up by transparent glass fanlights that filter gentle light into the interior.

A black marble staircase leads to the gym and sauna on the mezzanine floor. The restaurant and conference rooms are on the second floor, and all the remaining floors are devoted to guest rooms. Several features from the entrance hall are replicated in the rooms; for example, the reception-area pink appears on the glass panel separating sleeping quarters from the bathroom, wood (in this case, oak) is used throughout for the furniture and the floors, and Corian reappears in the bathrooms. The eighth floor is reserved for a special category of rooms, each of which has a balcony or private garden. To top it all off, from the wooden-deck terrace on the roof guests can enjoy the swimming pool and open-air bar while they admire the fine view of the Acropolis.

Architects: **Zeppos-Georgiadis+Associates**
Photography: **Fresh Hotel, C. Louisidis, K. Glinou**
Opening date: **2004**
Number of rooms: **133**
Address: **26 Sofokleous St, Athens, Greece**
Telephone: **+30 210 524 8511**
Fax: **+30 210 524 8517**
E-mail: **info@freshhotel.gr**
Web site: **www.freshhotel.gr**
Services: **bars, restaurant, conference rooms, gym, sauna, steam bath, swimming pool, roof terrace**

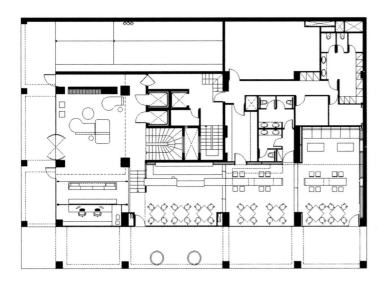

Ground-floor plan

Type plan

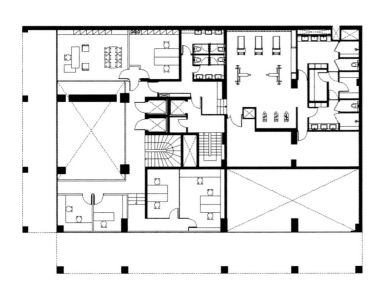

Mezzanine-floor plan

Roof plan

FAR FROM TOWN

SINGITA LEBOMBO

Located at the eastern edge of Kruger National Park in South Africa, near the border with Mozambique, Singita Lebombo is bounded by the most awe-inspiring scenery in the whole of Africa. The banks of the two rivers running through the approximately 37,000-acre parkland are the natural habitat for a surprising diversity of wildlife and vegetation.

The basis for this project was the supposition that guests would visit the lodge seeking experiences that were radically different from these of their normally stressful daily lives. However, there was a potential time constraint on the plan: the land occupied by the Lebombo might have to be returned to its original condition after 20 years. This factor greatly influenced the project, in that construction would need to be relatively lightweight and, above all, financially viable within the short time span.

Steering clear of the trend within contemporary African architecture, which is typically based on building thick adobe walls with thatched roofs, an alternative proposal was developed that explored more ethereal and spiritual ideas relating to the continent's identity, rituals, and beliefs. The architects resolved to convey the impermanence of human life by affirming our true scale within the context of our environment and disregarding our power to change nature.

These ideas were carried out by building a lodge with a minimal environmental impact. Using wood, glass, and steel as basic materials, the platforms on which the 15 suites are positioned appear to float in the space between the earth and the sky. Large glass screens protect the rooms from the wild animals and the scorching heat, while cane awnings and smaller screens provide shade and privacy, as well as reducing the visibility of the complex in the surrounding landscape. The transparency and starkness of the setting make the Lebombo a place for humans to commune with nature.

Architects: **Andrew Makin/omm design workshop, Joy Brasler**
Designers: **Cecile and Boyd's Interior Design**
Photography: **Singita Lebombo**
Opening date: **2003**
Number of rooms: **15**
Address: **Singita Lebombo, Kruger National Park, South Africa**
Telephone. **+27 21 683 3424**
Fax: **+27 21 683 3502**
E-mail: **reservations@singita.co.za**
Web site: **www.singita.com**
Services: **bar, restaurant, gym, spa, library, wine cellar, swimming pool**

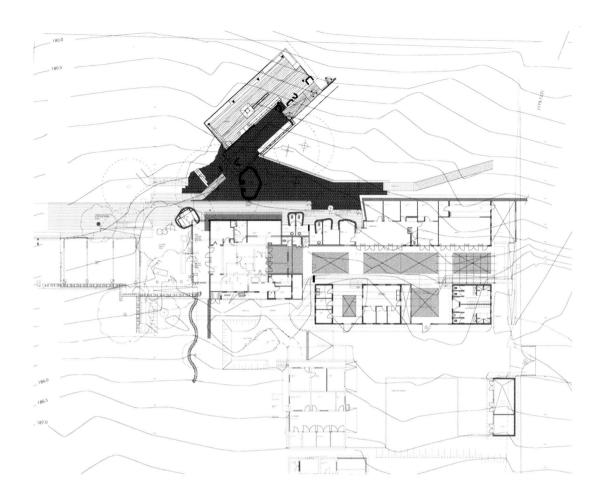

Main lodge floor plan

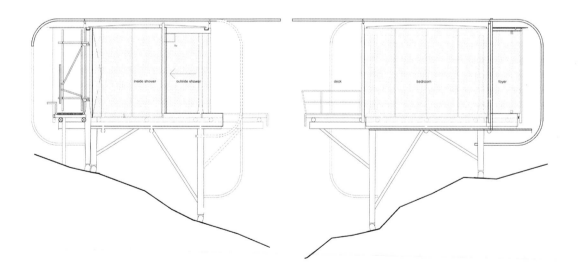

Cliff unit elevations

PERGOLA RESIDENCE

In the Pergola Residence, Matteo Thun, an architect from the Italian South Tirol region, fulfilled his desire to break away from the traditional one-family house and in its place bring into being his personal vision of integration with the environment: "Observe the beauty of nature and base your building on that." His capacity to recognize what is genuine led him to make use of natural materials such as wood, stone, and glass and to design a group of buildings with open views across the Adigio valley that are symbolic of the new Tirolean lifestyle dedicated to nature.

The Pergola Residence, situated about 1,200 feet up a sloping hillside, is composed of 12 residential units accessed from inside a wood-paneled gallery. Arranged on four floors, the apartments each contain a living room, a kitchen, and one or two bedrooms. The interiors are characterized by unpretentious and timeless linear design in which warm colors and wood prevail, with different finishes depending on the function. Large glass sliding doors open onto private balconies, that face south and are covered by the pergola that gives the establishment its name. At one end of the ground floor are the lobby, bar, and restaurant, and at the other end, the swimming pool, sauna, and adjoining terraces.

By eliminating all superfluous decorative elements and adhering to simplicity of form, the Pergola apartments allow visitors to pay attention to what really matters. Thun accomplishes a real change from the conventional architectural style of his birthplace with this return to nature that enhances the harmonious perception of the beauty of the surrounding landscape.

Architect: **Matteo Thun**
Photography: **Pergola Residence**
Opening date: **2004**
Number of rooms: **12**
Address: **St Kassianweg 40, Via S. Cassiano, Algund, South Tirol, Italy**
Telephone: **+39 0473 20 14 35**
Fax: **+39 0473 20 14 19**
E-mail: **info@pergola-residence.it**
Web site: **www.pergola-residence.it**
Services: **bar, indoor pool, sauna, private terraces**

PERGOLA
RESIDENCE

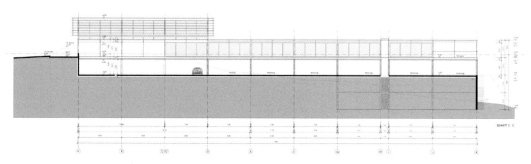

Elevation

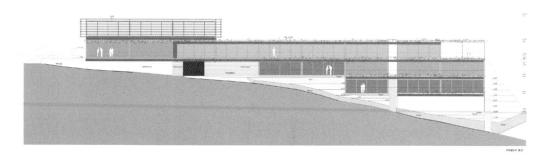

Elevation

Elegant, uncluttered interior design in the lounge at the Pergola Residence offers guests a meeting place completely surrounded by nature.

GRAND CAFÉ AND ROOMS

Plettenberg Bay, on South Africa's southern coast, is a small town on the Garden Route, that connects some of the country's most beautiful southeastern landscapes. Demolition of the old building on the site known as The Grand gave fashion designer Gail Behr the go-ahead for her major project.

The Grand was opened after just six months. Several factors dictated the nature of this building: space limitations; the desire to create a warm, inviting ambience for solitary travelers; Behr's wish to express her femininity throughout the building, where curves do indeed take precedence over straight lines; and finally, the need to incorporate several sets of very tall louvered doors acquired from a Bombay cricket club, which determined the height of the floors in certain places.

The hotel entrance leads directly to the bar and restaurant, while the reception area has been omitted altogether. The bar and adjacent terrace are the core of the hotel. From this central terrace, guests enjoy magnificent views of the surrounding ocean, mountains, and lake. The plain polished-concrete walls, floors, and ceilings mix well with the eclectic furnishings in warm shades and textures. Each of the eight rooms has a unique layout and a different décor. Those on the ground floor are situated next to the swimming pool, while first-floor rooms command splendid views of the surroundings.

This boutique hotel is a contemporary reinterpretation of the traditional family hotel. Its small size and limited capacity guarantee highly personalized service directly from the hotel's designer and manager. For Behr, the process of designing a hotel is similar to creating a new garment, with the sole exception that The Grand is a project that will never be fully finished but permanently subject to modifications at the hand of its designer.

Designer: **Gail Behr**
Photography: **Jac de Villiers**
Opening date: **2004**
Number of rooms: **8**
Address: **27 Main Road, Plettenberg Bay, Cape Town, South Africa**
Telephone: **+27 44 533 3301**
Fax: **+27 44 533 3301**
E-mail: **concierge@thegrand.co.za**
Web site: **www.thegrand.co.za**
Services: **bar and restaurant, swimming pool**

For Gail Behr, the driving force behind The Grand, spaces must necessarily grow and change progressively, which is why hotel rooms and communal areas are given an eclectic style in response to her own view of interior design.

HOTEL CASTELL

Hotel Castell was opened in 1913, only a few years after tourists began to realize the Alps were something more than just a remote locale inhabited by country folk. At an altitude of 6,175 feet, the original hotel built by Nicolaus Hartmann was fully renovated and extended in 2004. UN Studio, a Dutch firm of architects, undertook the greater part of this project, including building a new wing of 14 apartments and a Turkish bath, and renovating the entrance hall and 25 of the original rooms. Swiss architect Hans-Jörg Ruch refurbished another nine rooms, while Japanese architect Tadashi Kawamata designed the new oak-and-pine terrace surrounding Castell's original structure.

UN Studio took great pains to find the ideal location for the new apartment wing—Chesa Chastlatsch—in relation to the monolithic Hotel Castell and the surrounding landscape. The exterior of the building blends with the characteristics of the terrain as a result of the alternating jutting and embedded balconies on the façade, underlined by clear horizontal breaks reminiscent of tectonic plates. The east-west orientation means every room has a window facing south, and access to the best views is guaranteed through the large glazed surfaces on the main façade. The widespread use of glass, metal, and concrete surfaces emphasizes the modern conception of the new block, in contrast to the original 1913 construction. Since the main priority was to take maximum advantage of the panoramic views, a simple, open floor plan was selected for the apartments, allowing additional partitions to be easily put in place from a fixed central point.

The Turkish bath in the east-wing basement of the original building adheres to traditional design criteria, with a large, central paving-stone patio lit by several translucent glass cylinders that mark out different spaces, identifying the routes from both communal and private resting areas.

Architects: **UN Studio, Hans-Jörg Ruch**
Photography: **Christian Richters**
Opening date: **2004**
Number of rooms: **66**
Address: **CH-7524, Zuoz, Switzerland**
Telephone: **+41 (0) 81 851 5253**
Fax: **+41 (0) 81 851 5254**
E-mail: **info@hotelcastell.ch**
Web site: **www.hotelcastell.ch**
Services: **bar, restaurants, Turkish bath, terrace, swimming pool, ice rink, outdoor sauna**

CASTELL
THE FINE ART OF RELAXING

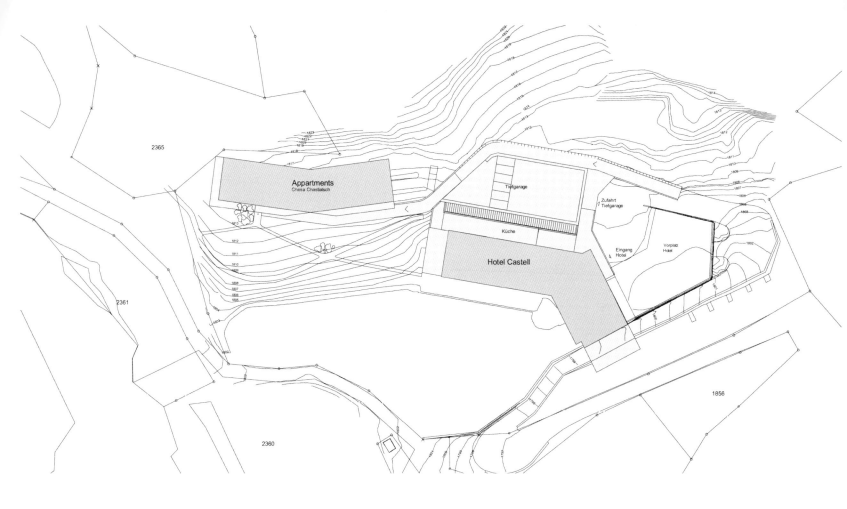

Site plan

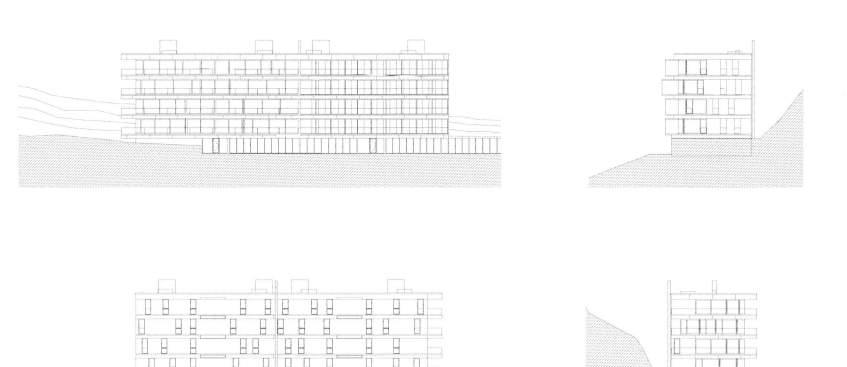

Elevations

142

Architect Gabrielle Hächler has compared the bar renovation at the Castell to a heart transplant. With her contribution, this twentieth-century hotel has acquired a healthy new organ. Space flows around the bright red bar, contrasting with the cold, white exterior.

MANDARIN ORIENTAL DHARA DHEVI

Located in northern Thailand in a beautiful setting of rice fields and tropical forests, Mandarin Oriental Dhara Dhevi offers a smart alternative to the tumult of Bangkok. The resort's architecture is strongly influenced by the rich cultural heritage of Chiang Mai, capital city of the Lanna Empire, which had its apogee between the thirteenth and sixteenth centuries.

Mandarin Oriental Dhara Dhevi is a living museum, where traditional Lanna culture merges with the splendor of the Asian colonial period to create a sophisticated and harmonious atmosphere. Architect Rachen Intawong traveled extensively throughout the Mekong region and became thoroughly acquainted with the area's traditional architecture. His team reinterpreted the theme of the majestic Lanna Imperial city, consisting of a central palace surrounded by separate groups of rice granaries.

Within a complex of 60 acres of tropical vegetation and water lily lakes, 64 villas and pavilions complement the main building, which includes 80 suites. The design of the pavilions is influenced by the indigenous architectural style, with sloping tile roofs and an abundance of local teak woodwork. The villas are based on the typical design of granaries found in the north of the country, while the residential suites offer the opulence of the old colonial hotels that were built throughout southeastern Asia during the nineteenth century. The common feature of all these types of accommodation is the sumptuous interior design, combining teak, stonework, mosaic, Thai silk, and marble as well as specially commissioned items from local artists and craftspeople, along with numerous antiques to add the finishing touches. The spa, which is a tourist destination in its own right, replicates the famous Mandalay palace in Myanmar.

The architects' wish to recover the vanished heritage of the Lanna kingdom distinguishes Mandarin Oriental Dhara Dhevi, surpassing the conventional concept of a resort and immersing guests in the splendor of a bygone Asian era.

Architects: **Nadadhorn Dhamabutra, Rachen Intawong**
Photography: **Mandarin Oriental Dhara Dhevi, Chiang Mai**
Opening date: **2004**
Number of rooms: **64 villas and 80 suites**
Address: **51/4 Moo 1, Chiang Mai-Sankampaeng Road, T. Tasala, A. Muang, Chiang Mai, Thailand**
Telephone: **+66 53 888 888**
Fax: **+66 53 888 999**
E-mail: **mocnx-enquiry@mohg.com**
Web site: **www.mandarinoriental.com**
Services: **spa, fitness center, tennis and squash courts, restaurants, shops, conference rooms, library**

Mandarin Oriental Dhara Dhevi offers a choice of four restaurants, each specializing in a different cuisine. Their interiors have been designed in accordance with the dishes served. Top: The Rice Terrace.

The work of a large team of craftspeople was required to build this hotel, which reflects the magnificent Lanna architecture and used many almost-forgotten traditional techniques.

NEW ARCHITECTURE

HOTEL ON RIVINGTON

During the nineteenth century, the Lower East Side of Manhattan was settled by immigrants, who occupied the distinctive brick buildings, each with its respective fire escape. Over the last few decades, the area has witnessed a transformation, becoming a haven for artists, restaurants, and fashionable stores. Capitalizing on this change, the Hotel on Rivington was envisaged more in terms of the future than based on the area's history. With this in mind, architects Grzywinski Pons and interior designer India Mahdavi were approached.

The aluminium-and-glass structure of the Hotel on Rivington contrasts vividly with the almost repetitive appearance of the neighboring five- and six-story apartment buildings. Its 21 stories fulfill a double function: to be a major player in the city skyline and to offer guests a magnificent view when they cross the threshold of each room. The hotel was conceived both from the inside out, and from the outside in: The partitioning of its glass superstructure determines the interior arrangement, and vice versa. One of its more outstanding features is the interaction between the building, the city, and the guests. The transparency of the structure offers guests the possibility of becoming a part of New York's landscape. The radical nature of the exposure of the interior of the hotel is extenuated by the arrangement of translucent glass in strategic points around the façade: opaque windows on the lower floors give way to totally transparent rooms as one rises toward the roof. In order to safeguard guests' privacy, the architects installed a system of automatic blinds that provide complete seclusion in a matter of seconds.

With the exception of the surprising ground-floor lobby and restaurant designed by the Dutch architect Marcel Wanders, the interior is predominantly characterized by straight lines and restrained sumptuousness. The bar, restaurant, and lounge are found on the lower floor, while the guest rooms occupy the remaining floors.

Architects: **Grzywinski Pons Architects**
Photography: **Floto+Warner**
Opening date: **2005**
Number of rooms: **110**
Address: **107 Rivington Street, New York, New York, United States**
Telephone: **+1 212 475 2600**
Fax: **+1 212 475 5959**
E-mail: **info@hotelonrivington.com**
Web site: **www.hotelonrivington.com**
Services: **bar, restaurant, library, conference room, in-room spa services**

Marcel Wanders designed the ground-floor public areas, with the sweeping,
red-carpeted entrance hall, where white clouds appear to float on the walls
and ceilings.

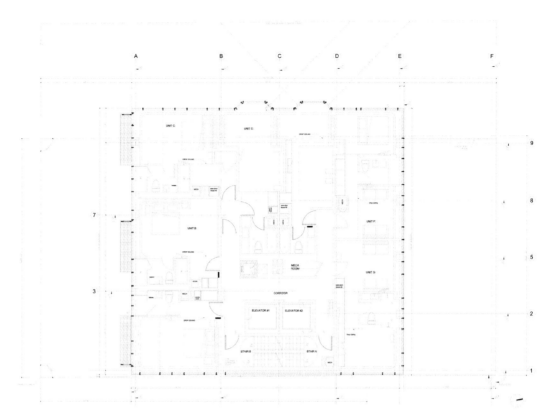

Type-floor plan

Penthouse

Glass walls enclose the bedroom and the bathroom, giving guests the sensation of floating high up in the Big Apple.

HOTEL DIAGONAL BARCELONA

Hotel Diagonal Barcelona stands at the northern end of one of the city's main arteries, next to Jean Nouvel's impressive Agbar tower. Recognizing the impossibility of escaping the visual influence of Nouvel's construction, Juli Capella and his team proposed a building that would act as a backdrop to the tower, avoiding any communion between the two. Against Nouvel's colorful cylinder, this hotel displays a prismatic form in black and white.

The longitudinal prism has upright stone projections on the façade that stand out like white keys against the dark glass. On the east and west façades, white concrete trays point up the flooring slabs and denote the number of floors. The façade facing Nouvel's tower is composed of large projections covering several stories at a time, and the façade looking out onto the private gardens is structured as three volumes with a cantilevered shelf at the top and two large canopies.

The ground floor was inspired by the idea of a large aquarium; an undulating roof in a circular pattern symbolizes the water surface. On the floor—submerged in the fishbowl, as it were—are the reception, lounge, bar, and restaurant areas. The restaurant sits opposite the main entrance hall, at the other end of the ground level, accentuating the pointed shape of the floor plan. It commands wonderful views of the gardens.

All 240 rooms, distributed on 10 floors, communicate via corridors illuminated by gentle, bluish light. One type of room has direct views to the exterior through large windows, while the view from the other type is sheltered by the projections on the façade. This space permits a writing desk and a lounge area to be added to the bedroom. Corner rooms offer truly stunning views. All the main hotel facilities are on the roof level, including a vast wooden terrace with swimming pool and bar.

Architects: **Juli Capella, Miquel Garcia/Capella Garcia Arquitectura**
Photography: **Rafael Vargas**
Opening date: **2005**
Number of rooms: **240**
Address: **Avda. Diagonal 205, Barcelona, Spain**
Telephone: **+34 934 895 300**
Fax: **+34 934 895 309**
E-mail: **hotel.diagonalbcn@hoteles-silken.com**
Web site: **www.hoteldiagonalbarcelona.com**
Services: **bar, restaurant, conference rooms, roof terrace, swimming pool**

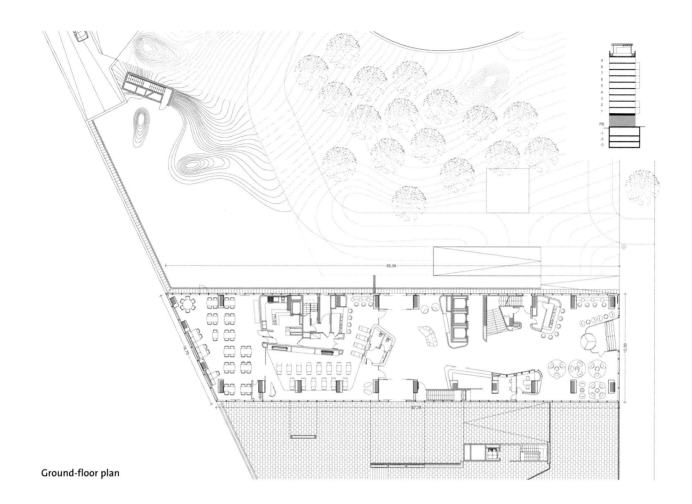

Ground-floor plan

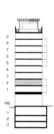

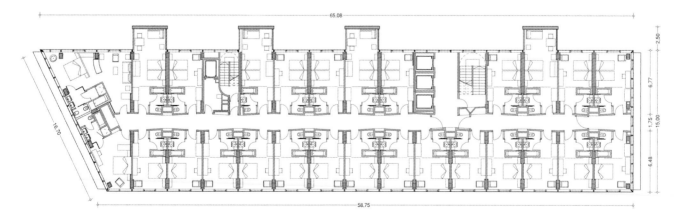

Type-floor plan

The ground-floor area was designed to resemble a giant glass aquarium and contains all the necessary services, presented as submerged volumes with different surfaces: copper, wood, glazed-tile mosaics, pebbles, and so on.

PARKHOTEL HALL

Hall in Tirol is a medieval town in the western foothills of the Alps, only 5 miles from Innsbruck. By 1931, the growing tourist interest in the area had led the Austrian architect Lois Welzenbacher to design the Hotel Seeber. The initial construction was a seven-story structure with projecting balconies arranged to give a rotating movement to the building, capped by a glass roof. After several decades of improvements and extensions and by the year 2000, the hotel had lost its idiosyncrasy due to the disappearance of the balconies and the original roof. A year later, Henke und Schreieck won a competition to improve and extend the new Parkhotel, successor to the Seeber.

The Austrian architects' goal was first to eliminate all additions to the original building in order to restore it, in keeping with its classification as a modern edifice, and bringing out the singularity of the original construction. To resolve the structural problems, it was necessary to rebuild the staircase. A tower was designed, which, through its form and positioning, resembles the old Seeber. Both buildings independently achieved their own identity as products of their time.

The new building sits on a long, completely transparent base. It is one story high and comprises the reception area and public space, which unites the two volumes. The tower, which becomes progressively wider as it rises, takes the form of a tinted glass structure that is protected from sun and rain by a series of eaves arranged around the topmost perimeter. The guest rooms, distributed among seven floors, are arranged around the central axis of the building in such a way that they all enjoy splendid views, thanks to the transparency of the tower.

Architects: **Henke und Schreieck**

Photography: **Bruno Klomfar**

Opening date: **2003**

Number of rooms: **59**

Address: **Thurnfeldgasse 1, 6060 Hall in Tirol, Austria**

Telephone: **+43 52 23 53 769**

Fax: **+43 52 23 54 653**

E-mail: **info@parkhotel-hall.com**

Web site: **www.parkhotel-hall.com**

Services: **bar, restaurant, conference rooms, roof terrace, sauna, gym, tennis court**

The lounge, at the base of the new cylindrical volume, is a vast, single-story area with practically no inner divisions, dedicated to communal spaces and extending beyond the original building.

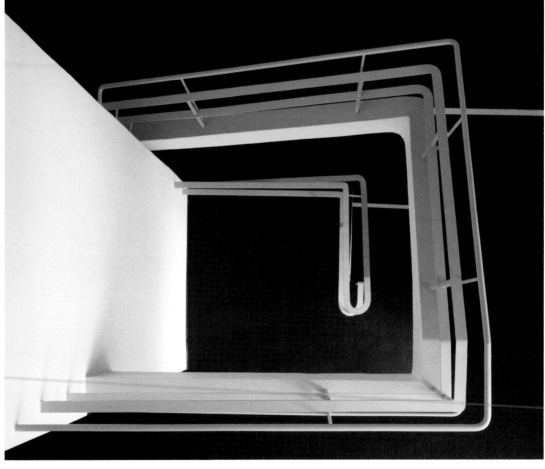

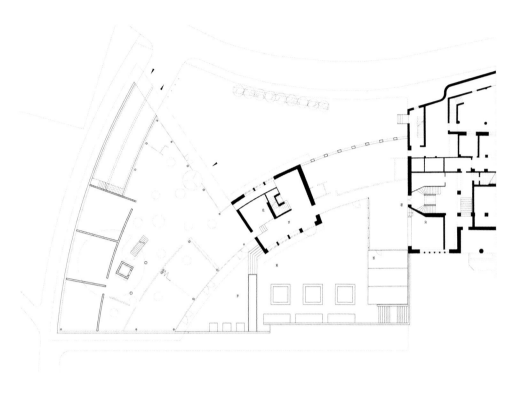

Ground-floor plan

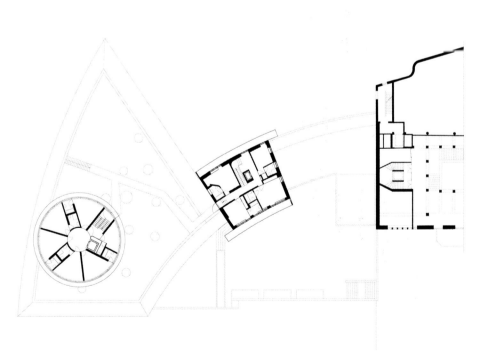

First-floor plan

HOTEL BARCELONA PRINCESS

This hotel is located at 1 Avenida Diagonal, the long avenue traced across the whole of Barcelona. At approximately 350 feet tall, the Barcelona Princess has taken its place in the city skyline from its privileged position on the Mediterranean seafront.

The site for this hotel gave the building its characteristic triangular plan and invited architects to design a project as emblematic for Barcelona as the Flatiron Building is for New York. The tower was divided into two in order to reduce its weight and at the same time accentuate the "ship's bow" image. A glass bridge joins the slender volumes, and a spectacular sliver of light is projected through the gap onto the avenue below. The blue-and-orange-stained concrete structure was given a polished-granite base at ground-floor level. Each façade has a spectacularly different surface material: Those facing Avenida Diagonal are dressed in opaque sheet aluminum, which conceals the individuality of the rooms inside, while the south face is a transparent glass surface with strips of both tinted glass and printed glass, providing protection from the sun without interrupting the view.

The ground floor is taken up mainly by the large, double-height lobby, where, as in the rest of the building, a selection of furniture by the leading names in current design is on view. The hall adjacent to the lobby, which is separated from it only by generous glass panels, was named Sala Dalí after the architect's friend, the famous Ampurdán painter. The transparent bridge between the two towers is wider at its base to accommodate several communal spaces, including a climatized outdoor swimming pool on the third floor. The splendid panoramic views from the large windows in each of the rooms are impressive, but they are particularly awe-inspiring from the bar and open-air swimming pool on the twenty-third floor, where the pool and the sea appear to merge.

Architects: **Arquitecturas Oscar Tusquets Blanca**
Photography: **Gunnar Knetchel, Rafael Vargas**
Opening date: **2004**
Number of rooms: **366**
Address: **Avda. Diagonal 1, Barcelona, Spain**
Telephone: **+34 933 561 000**
Fax: **+34 933 561 022**
E-mail: **bcn.reservas@princess-hotels.com**
Web site: **www.hotelbarcelonaprincess.com**
Services: **bars, restaurants, conference rooms, spa, gym, swimming pools, roof terrace**

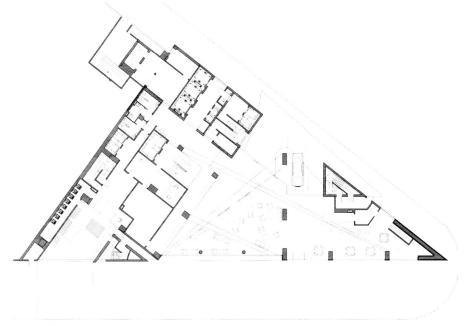

Ground-floor plan

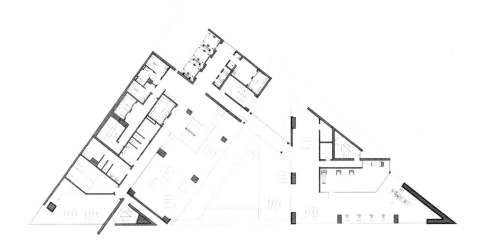

Third-floor plan

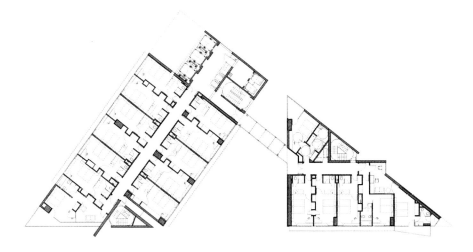

Type plan

Sala Dalí, hosting a permanent exhibition of the Ampurdán painter's tapestries, contains several Dalilips evolved from the first sofa designed by Dalí in 1936, inspired by the lips of actress Mae West.

HOTEL URBAN

Located within the financial, political, and cultural center of Madrid, Hotel Urban is an outstanding testament to the efforts of the architects to capture a new classic architectural style, designed to merge with the existing buildings and monuments within the surrounding cityscape.

From the façade, whose laminated steel outline is reminiscent of classic architecture, a glass tower rises, accommodating a number of suites. The apertures around the building are larger at the ground floor so as to identify the entrances, while at the top floor they come together into the pitched roof. A large canopied doorway leads into the corridor, consisting of an impressive combination of forms, energies, and light that contrasts with the wonderful New Guinea totem poles, that add a touch of the exotic to the space. Opposite the reception area, two panoramic elevators span the entire height of the building, illumined by a vertical alabaster light connecting the corridor with the glass roof. The ground floor also accommodates the Glass Bar, a reading area, and the restaurant. The same black Zimbabwe stone unifies the ground floor with the basement, where an antique art collection is housed, along with conference facilities.

The 96 rooms are divided among three standard floors surmounted by the attic, where guests may enjoy the solarium, the open-air restaurant, and the swimming pool. In the rooms, attention to detail and harmony of materials are enhanced by careful lighting. An undoubtedly unique feature of each room is the selection of Asian cultural objects used for ornamentation.

The close collaboration between architects and interior designers prevented the inconsistency sometimes found between these two functions. This cooperative work is evident in the material and conceptual harmony that exists between the outside and the interior of the building, which constitutes a new approach based on the features of historic 1930s architecture.

Architects: **Carles Bassó, Mariano Martitegui**
Designers: **Kim Castells, Jordi Cuenca**
Photography: **Ana Coello**
Opening date: **2004**
Number of rooms: **96**
Address: **Carrera de San Jerónimo 34, Madrid, Spain**
Telephone: **+34 917 877 770**
Fax: **+34 917 877 799**
E-mail: **urban@derbyhotels.com**
Web site: **www.derbyhotels.com**
Services: **wine cellar, sauna, gym, outdoor swimming pool, solarium, Egyptian museum, conference rooms**

A preacher's pulpit and a prayer seat from Oceania face the "Black Sun," a translucent circle of glass fitted in the black floor, through which light from the basement glows.

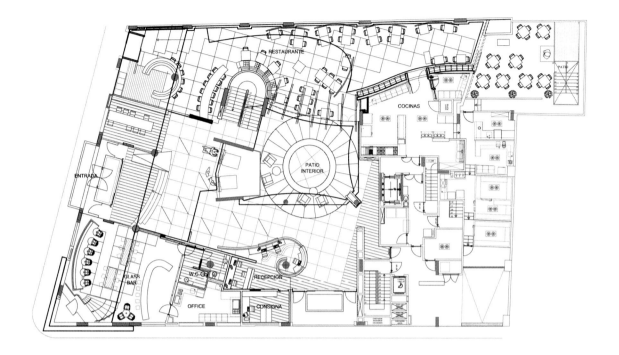

Ground-floor plan

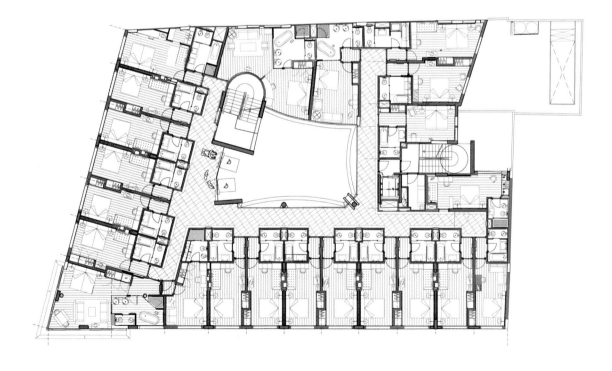

Type plan

Some of the hotel's suites are located in the glass tower that rises above the
cornice, highlighting the point where the two façades meet.

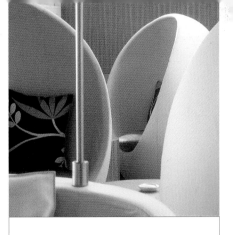

W SEOUL-WALKERHILL

On being challenged to design Asia's first six-star hotel, Studio Gaia designers decided to bring new meaning to the concept of a boutique hotel. Described as a sumptuous paradise with urban sensibilities, W Seoul-Walkerhill is outstanding as a result of its exclusive design, which involves a spectacular use of space and color. This project sought to combine the latest technology with the demands of comfort, resulting in a surprisingly luxurious and homey urban refuge. The careful design, which extends even to staff uniforms, includes a wide selection of works by local and international artists inviting guests to participate in the personal creative experience.

The imposing size of the entrance hall might be overbearing were it not for the interplay of light and shadow, creating a varied and sophisticated ambience. Guests relax here, amid the formal clarity, which is the hallmark of Studio Gaia projects, enjoying the splendid panoramic views of the river Han and the cityscape unfolding beyond the large windows.

The 253 rooms were designed according to four basic models: the Wonderful Room, a warm and attractive space combining red and white tones; the Spa Room, where gray and white contrast with wood, favorable to therapeutic relaxation; the Media Room, including the latest multimedia technology, where videos can be viewed from the generous round bed or the gigantic red bath; and the Scent Room, in which the effects of aromatherapy are enhanced by a placid white-and-blue interior opening onto a private balcony.

The ability of Studio Gaia to anticipate new trends while absorbing and interpreting contemporary culture and design was fundamental to accomplishing the W Hotel's brief: to offer establishments where harmonious, modern esthetics, free from traditional hotel clichés, are combined with maximum comfort for guests.

Design: **Studio Gaia**
Photographer: **W Seoul-Walkerhill, Studio Gaia**
Opening date: **2004**
Number of rooms: **253**
Address: **21 Gwangjang-dong, Gwangjin-gu, Seoul, South Korea**
Telephone: **+82 2 465 2222**
Fax: **+82 2 450 4989**
E-mail: **wseoul@whotels.com**
Web site: **www.whotels.com/seoul**
Services: **restaurants, bar, shops, hairdresser, gym**

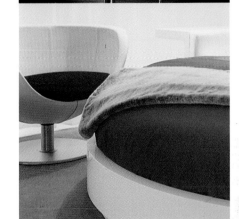

The huge communal spaces on the ground and first floors provide a wide choice of atmospheres for guests, whether they prefer to relax in suspended ovoid swing chairs, retreat into first-floor booths with a view onto the lounge below, or curl up by the fireplace to enjoy a magnificent view of the river Han.

Clean-cut lines, an exceptional lighting scheme, and dramatic chromatic contrasts characterize the bold, informal, contemporary design of W Seoul-Walkerhill, a hotel that strikes a happy medium between large hotel chains and smaller-scale boutique hotels.

HOTEL PUERTA AMÉRICA

Hotel Puerta América was a task of titanic proportions that required 19 world-renowned architecture and interior design studios to work together on a proposal for a hotel complex based on freedom of form and eclecticism. All of the floors share a basic layout consisting of a centrally placed lobby from which two corridors lead off to the rooms on either side. However, each offers a different interpretation of the "hotel" concept, displaying a seemingly endless variety of materials, colors, and shapes.

Located in the very heart of Madrid, this hotel is surrounded by carefully laid out gardens designed to screen the building from the surrounding urban activity. Paul Éluard's poem "Liberté" is the central motif of the main façade, designed by Jean Nouvel, where the verses are written in several languages and different colors on the sunshades protecting the building. The structure consists of two centrally adjacent cylinders giving rise to two wings of rooms.

The floor plans for the rooms were personalized to reflect each architect's individual style. Zaha Hadid favored liquid, fluent lines; Norman Foster created serene ambiences; David Chipperfield used startling combinations of light and color; Eva Castro and Holger Kehne assembled geometric figures; Victorio & Lucchino conferred warmth; Mark Newson used brilliant, shiny materials; Ron Arad sought to provoke; Kathryn Findlay produced a space for meditation; Richard Gluckman proposed transparent spaces with the lightness of polymethyl methacrylate; Arata Isozaki's proposals incorporated Japanese tradition; Javier Mariscal and Fernando Salas provided colorful graphic design features; and Jean Nouvel, who also designed the communal areas for the twelfth floor that command spectacular views over the city, contributed a hybrid between architecture and photography.

Architects and designers: **Ron Arad, Jonathan Bell, Harriet Bourne, Jason Bruges, Eva Castro, David Chipperfield, Kathryn Findlay, Norman Foster, Richard Gluckman, Zaha Hadid, Arata Isozaki, Holger Kehne, Christian Liaigre, Javier Mariscal, Mark Newson, Jean Nouvel, John Pawson, Felipe Sáez de Gordoa, Fernando Salas, Teresa Sapey, Victorio & Lucchino**
Photography: **Roger Casas**
Opening date: **2005**
Number of rooms: **342**
Address: **Avda. América 41, Madrid, Spain**
Telephone: **+34 917 445 400**
Fax: **+34 917 445 401**
E-mail: **hotel.puertamerica@hoteles-silken.com**
Web site: **www.hotelpuertamerica.com**
Services: **bar, restaurant, conference rooms, indoor swimming pool, sauna, terrace, garden**

The ground-floor communal areas and conference halls are the work of John Pawson, who, with few materials, has created an impressive space, enlarged and enhanced through the use of wood.

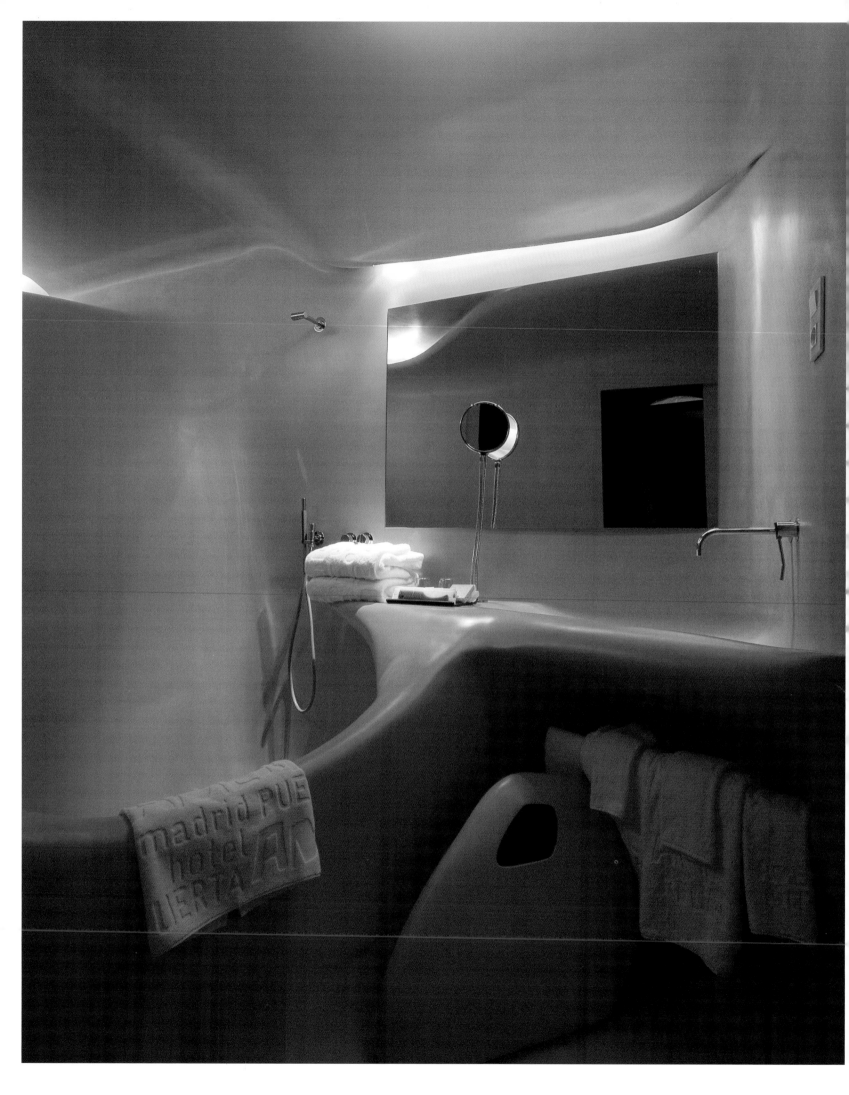

The rooms designed by Zaha Hadid, feel like something out of a science-fiction film: futuristic use of space in dazzling white and sinuous lines where the items of furniture merge into a single piece of LG HI-MACS acrylic.

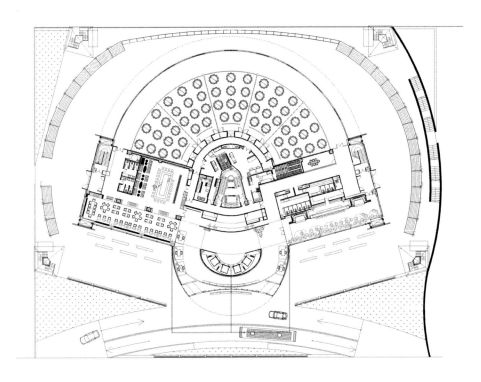

Ground-floor plan

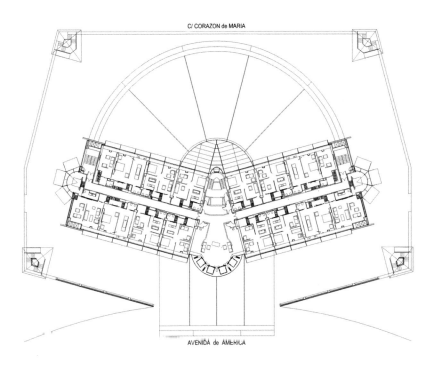

Type plan

NEW INTERIORS

The architect who undertakes the restoration of an old building faces the decision of how much of the building's past to preserve. Regardless of the building's previous use—brewery, consulate, prison, or private residence, just to cite a few examples from this chapter—the preservation of original architectural features gives the building a personality that is impossible to create without affectation or artificiality in an entirely new construction. Nevertheless, the merit of the hotels described here is not only in knowing what to preserve, but also in knowing how to juxtapose old and new so as to offer a unique experience, both for the

EAST HOTEL

Before being restored to its present condition as the East Hotel, this building was an abandoned iron foundry near the theater and club district along Hamburg's Reeperbahn. Since its opening at the end of 2004, the hotel has become a meeting place for sophisticated guests and their companions, who have made the East Hotel into a nerve center of night and day life in the area.

The hotel consists of two distinct volumes. The old foundry contains 12 rooms built above the main restaurant, which specializes in Asian cuisine. The restaurant communicates with the luxurious interior garden via several imposing glass doors that are over 20 feet tall. A spectacular wall sculpture screens the cellar, where smaller groups of diners can be seated, as well as a bar furnished with ottomans. The Smirnoff Lounge is accessed by means of a beautiful staircase and offers a splendid overlook of the restaurant space, which itself is more than 30 feet tall. A bar that is almost 65 feet long runs the entire length of the main dining area, toward the reception area, and also outside onto the terrace overlooking the garden. The remainder of the rooms are arranged inside a second building, along with the conference rooms and the spa.

The main building's industrial past influenced the project's designers, who were also inspired by the fusion of eastern and western cultures and by the conviction that public spaces should display a healthy measure of idiosyncrasy combined with an inner logic similar to that encountered in poetry or dreams. This combination of ideas led to the particular choice of forms, some of which were achieved by using molds shaped like gigantic raindrops and Thai cowbells; the use of vivid colors typical of Indian spices, flowers, and silks; the contrast between forms and materials; the sudden changes in level; and the simultaneous sensation of familiarity and strangeness stimulated by certain characteristics of the building.

Architects: **Jordan Mozer & Associates**
Photography: **Doug Snower**
Opening date: **2004**
Number of rooms: **103**
Address: **31 Simon von Utrecht Strasse, Hamburg, Germany**
Telephone: **+49 40 30 99 30**
Fax: **+49 40 30 99 32 00**
E-mail: **info@east-hamburg.de**
Web site: **www.east-hamburg.de**
Services: **bars, restaurants, conference rooms, sauna, spa, gym, outdoor putting green, roof terrace**

The East Hotel is arranged around a large central space, some 36 feet high, joined to the inner patio through four massive glass doors.

The interior of this former foundry features new paintings and sculptures depicting imaginary forms achieved through the combination of the latest information technologies and traditional artistic techniques.

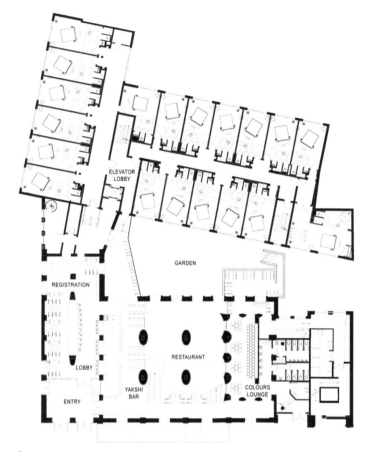

Ground-floor plan

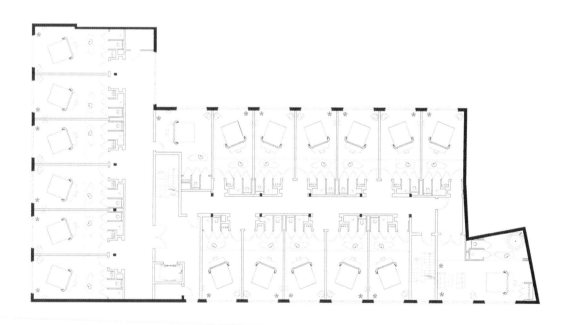

Type plan

LLOYD HOTEL

The Lloyd Hotel is located within the Amsterdam port district, which has seen a profound redevelopment in recent decades. Over the past century, the property's disruptive history—between 1920 and 1930 it was an immigration center, then a prison from 1941 to 1989, and finally, between 1989 and 1999, headquarters for various arts-and-crafts workshops—led to a general deterioration of the building's interior, although the façade and general structure were undisturbed by the ravages of time and successive occupancies. The bid to build a hotel offering rooms at various quality levels, a restaurant open to the neighboring community, and a "cultural embassy" was the successful entry in a competition held toward the end of the 1990s by the Amsterdam City Council to find a new purpose for the building.

Rotterdam architects MVRDV undertook the refurbishment of the Lloyd Hotel, starting with the premise that the ill-fated edifice's troubled history had to be overcome, then accentuating the open spaces and using a good measure of ingenuity to complete the project. Rooms were envisaged not only as sleeping quarters, but also as places in which to relax or work, and to this end, numerous designers and artists were invited to collaborate in the project's development.

At the heart of the original Lloyd Hotel building was a large open space reaching from the basement to the roof, covered by a glass top. The new restaurant is situated where the three previous dining areas were located, and various areas dedicated to the activities of the cultural embassy were suspended within the large open space. The embassy serves as a link between residents and the city's artistic life and, in collaboration with the Lloyd Hotel, organizes cultural projects and events. Scattered throughout the building are reminders of the Lloyd's earlier history, such as the glazed tile walls, glasswork with nautical imagery, and wooden booths where emigrants purchased their passage to America.

Architects: **MVRDV**
Photography: **Rob't Hart**
Opening date: **2004**
Number of rooms: **116**
Address: **Oostelijke Handelskade 34, Amsterdam, Netherlands**
Telephone: **+31 20 561 3636**
Fax: **+31 20 561 3600**
E-mail: **post@lloydhotel.com**
Web site: **www.lloydhotel.com**
Services: **restaurant, terrace, conference rooms, cultural embassy, library, music room, shop**

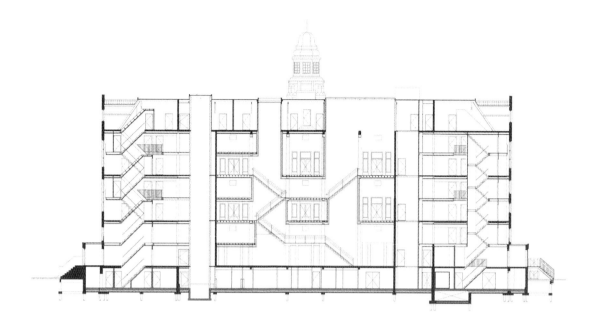

Longitudinal section

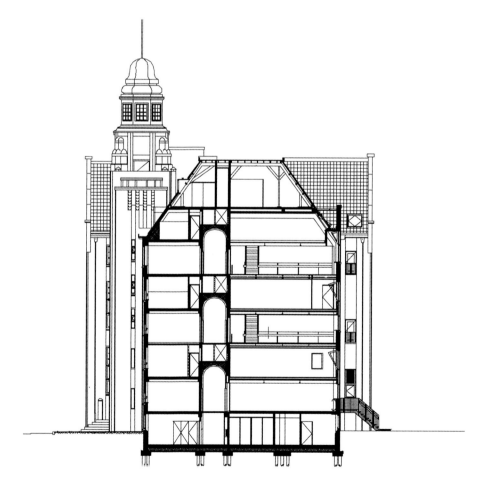

Cross section

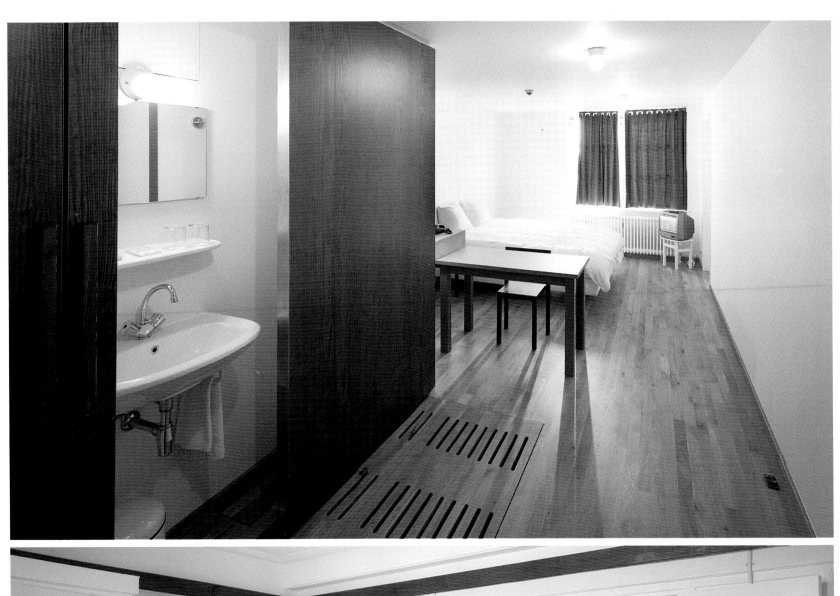

Some of the 116 rooms have been refurbished, while others are newly built, but all are ranked on a category scale from one to five stars, depending on the dimensions of their floor plan.

In the new rooms, the traditional entrance and hallway with a bathroom on one side was eliminated in favor of a single space comprising bathing and sleeping quarters.

FAENA HOTEL AND UNIVERSE

Located between central Buenos Aires and the adjoining nature reserve, the El Porteño building has for over a century been emblematic of the Puerto Madero quarter. The collaboration between Alan Faena and Philippe Starck resulted in a metropolitan oasis based on a new concept and way of life in the hospitality business.

Having already successfully completed various other establishments, Starck's team designed a hotel experience based on three criteria: majestic setting, rich and diverse content, and warmth of service. Refurbishing El Porteño entailed transforming the seven-story building into a hotel as well as 85 apartments. The premise behind the whole project was the quest for luxury and comfort, with abundant use of fine natural materials such as Tuscany marble and native lapacho lumber, as well as Starck's distinctively oversized baths, chandeliers, and etched glass.

The hotel entrance, some 30 feet high, leads visitors into the Transformative Way, a long and lavishly carpeted corridor luxuriously accessorized with etched glass and red and gold imperial velvet curtains. This romantic, regal style is maintained throughout the 83 bedrooms, noteworthy for the bold and extravagant taste they showcase. Although Starck designed eight different types of room, they share common features such as velvet curtains, fantastic views, and glass partitions between the bedroom and the bathroom richly appointed in marble.

In accordance with the wish of Faena and Starck to create a hotel establishment on a human scale, an entire universe has been conjured up, inviting guests to go beyond the boundaries of a traditional hotel and experience the cabaret, the gymnasium, and even a tango dancing school.

Designer: **Philippe Starck**
Photography: **Nikolas Koenig**
Opening date: **2004**
Number of rooms: **83**
Address: **Martha Salotti 445, Puerto Madero Este, Buenos Aires, Argentina**
Telephone: **+54 11 4010 9000**
Fax: **+54 11 4010 9001**
E-mail: **info@faenaexperience.com**
Web site: **www.faenahotelanduniverse.com**
Services: **restaurants, outdoor terrace, business center, gym-Turkish bath, swimming pool, pool bar, shop, beauty center**

Philippe Starck proposed a romantic, imperial style for the Universe, a complex of communal spaces for showcasing art, fashion, and entertainment.

PALAU DE LA MAR

PALAU DE LA MAR

Palau de la Mar, in Valencia's Eixample district, is just a footstep away from the historic heart of this Mediterranean city currently in the midst of a profound urban regeneration process.

This project entailed converting two adjacent, listed buildings into a hotel. The more outstanding of the original constructions was a mid-nineteenth-century mansion with an off-white façade adorned with wrought iron balconies and marine and floral motifs, artfully preserved and restored. The other, a red ochre mansion, is clearly distinguished from the first, but inside, both spaces have been merged into a single unit through masterly interior design and seamless horizontal communication on each floor.

The original arched and vaulted carriage doorway, typical of nineteenth-century mansions, has been kept as a porched entrance to the hotel. This vast portal leads to a magnificent marble staircase, a hallmark of the new hotel, which was renovated in order to use this powerful visual feature to unify the original spaces according to the proposed plan. Guest rooms are of different sizes and shapes, but the underlying esthetic criteria for materials and finishes—wengue wood flooring, furniture based on essential geometric shapes, and marble veneer in the bathrooms—ensures continuity throughout.

The minimalist interior patio, in contrast to the noble air of classicism pervading the rest of the edifice, constitutes one of the central spaces in Palau de la Mar, emphasising the establishment's desire to represent the culture of the city and its citizens. Every species of flora planted here, with Valencia's emblematic orange blossom taking the place of honor, is deeply rooted in Mediterranean culture. Surrounding this patio, a lightweight, two-story wood-and-glass extension was erected. The basement accommodates a spa, designed to follow the same straight lines and simple forms used throughout the entire hotel.

Architects: **Hospes Design**
Photography: **Hospes**
Opening date: **2004**
Number of rooms: **66**
Address: **Av. Navarro Reverter 14, Valencia, Spain**
Telephone: **+34 963 162 884**
Fax: **+34 963 162 885**
E-mail: **palaudelamar@hospes.es**
Web site: **www.hospes.es**
Services: **bar, restaurant, conference rooms, library, gym, sauna, spa, swimming pool, interior patio**

The architectural singularity of Palau de la Mar is protected under a special plan that values the entrance hallway and main staircase in particular as the most representative elements of these former stately homes.

THE THREE SISTERS HOTEL

The Three Sisters Hotel is situated at the intersection of Pikk and Tolli streets, in the historic district of Tallinn. The three adjoining houses that inspired the name of this hotel and were originally built in the fourteenth century, are an architectural grouping of immense cultural and historic interest, which for decades had been calling out for complete restoration.

In spite of their relatively uniform exterior, the three buildings are quite different in character on the inside. The larger "Big Sister," right at the crossroad, has a rectangular floor plan, while the other two sisters are more eye-catching inside, despite their modest façades. The "Middle Sister" consists of a large central room next to the kitchen and bath. The atypical arrangement of the "Little Sister" is dominated by an inner courtyard onto which the adjoining rooms open. The architects' and designers' brief called for in taking advantage of the uniqueness of the original buildings to build a hotel that combines classicism with modernity.

THE THREE SISTERS

The main entrance in the "Middle Sister" leads into a large hallway which was created by removing part of the upper floor. The library is to the left, and beyond the bar and restaurant is the Angels Room, a cozy space decorated with eighteenth-century frescoes and offering a view into the adjoining courtyard. The design of the rooms was influenced by the building's architectural legacy. "Big Sister" is better suited to traditionally styled rooms; "Middle Sister" contains large, individually laid-out rooms and "Little Sister" is divided between rooms that open on the inner courtyard and those that overlook the street.

The restoration of many original architectural features, such as stairs, arches, and beams, allowed the idiosyncrasies of "Three Sisters" to be not only preserved but also enhanced, providing a contrast to the unobtrusive lines of contemporary Scandinavian design.

Architect: **Martinus Schuurman**
Designer: **Külli Salum**
Photography: **The Three Sisters Hotel, Martinus Schuurman**
Opening date: **2003**
Number of rooms: **23**
Address: **Pikk 71/Tolli 2, Tallinn, Estonia**
Telephone: **+372 6 306 300**
Fax: **+372 6 306 301**
E-mail. **info@threesistershotel.com**
Web site: **www.threesistershotel.com**
Services: **bar, restaurant, wine cellar, library, inner courtyard**

Despite preserving numerous original structural elements, the buildings'
interior layout was substantially altered in order to optimize horizontal communication among all three spaces.

Cross section

HOTEL SON BRULL

Reflecting Majorca's turbulent history, Son Brull has been subjected to many different uses since it was built in the twelfth century. This building at the foot of a hill near the village of Pollença was a Moorish dairy farm during the Middle Ages. Later, the Desbrull family made it their residence; in 1745, it was converted into a Jesuit monastery and was given its present form; and finally, after King Charles III expelled the Jesuits from Spain, it became a private residence once again.

The plan hinges on the typically Mediterranean central patio, from which access to the entrance hall, the restaurant, the bar, and a conference hall is gained. All 23 guest rooms were arranged on the mezzanine, second, and third floors. In the vestibule in front of the restaurant, a wall-length fireplace commands an array of black easy chairs and gold-colored arched reading lamps. In the dining room, the fine gold-leaf finish on the tray ceiling is a striking contrast to the stone walls and arches. The bar is built into a nineteenth-century oil press. The huge pieces of machinery used for pressing olives have been preserved and displayed. At one end of the rectangular floor plan is the bar, which is made of iron and veneered with wood from the trunk of a pine tree. At the other end is the lounge area. The bar opens onto the outdoor restaurant, which is protected by an iron-and-cane pergola. This area extends to the teak-floored solarium and swimming pool. Each room is different in terms of size and layout, but all share a similar interior atmosphere because of the furnishings, which were designed largely by the architects themselves.

Preserving the building's original architectural features, Ignasi Forteza has completely transformed the property, bringing together in harmonious style the latest trends, Majorcan traditional values, and the historical traces of the monastery in this hotel project.

Architects: **Forteza Carbonell Associats**
Photography: **Eugeni Pons**
Opening date: **2003**
Number of rooms: **23**
Address: **Son Brull, Pollença, Majorca, Spain**
Telephone: **+34 971 535 353**
Fax: **+34 971 531 068**
E-mail: **info@sonbrull.com**
Web site: **www.sonbrull.com**
Services: **bar, restaurant, library, conference rooms, spa, tennis court, swimming pools, garden**

Black makes a strong impression in this space dominated by stone walls and gilt ceilings: the dining room is joined to a vestibule by means of a black lacquered cabinet unit, and matching benches order the array of tables.

HOTEL DU VIN

Henley, situated on the river Thames, west of London, is steeped in local history. In the mid-eighteenth-century, the Brakspears brewery opened for business just a few yards from the riverbanks, flourishing until 2004. Starting with the Georgian building that once housed the brewery, architect Michael Phillips and his team embarked on this project intending to capitalize on the building's industrial past and its central location.

The architects' wish was to keep the original structure of the building intact, implying some restrictions on the partitioning of the space, which was limited to light dividing walls and glass screens. The brewery had been organized around a central courtyard, which was preserved and transformed into a central open space around which the main communal areas of the hotel were grouped.

The current hotel entrance was once the entry to the brewery. The ground floor features a reception area, bar, and double-height restaurant. The wine cellar is visible from the passageway running between the bar and the restaurant, and additional openings were created to connect with the restaurant. The lobby is located next to the restaurant, and beyond that, in the oldest part of the building, is the billiard room.

Nine of the 43 guest rooms can be accessed directly from the central court-yard, affording guests the greatest degree of privacy. In many of the rooms, the peculiar structure of the brewery permitted some unique design features and double-height spaces, proving that with careful planning, the atmosphere and idiosyncrasies of an older building are not necessarily a handicap, but can be made an advantage.

Architect: **Mike Phillips**
Photography: **Dan Duchars**
Opening date: **2005**
Number of rooms: **43**
Address: **Brakspears Brewery, New Street, Henley-on-Thames, United Kingdom**
Telephone: **+44 149 184 8400**
Fax: **+44 149 184 8401**
E-mail: **info@henley.hotelduvin.com**
Web site: **www.hotelduvin.com**
Services: **bar, restaurant, billiard room and cigar gallery, conference rooms, wine cellar, inner courtyard**

Hotel du Vin
&
Bistro

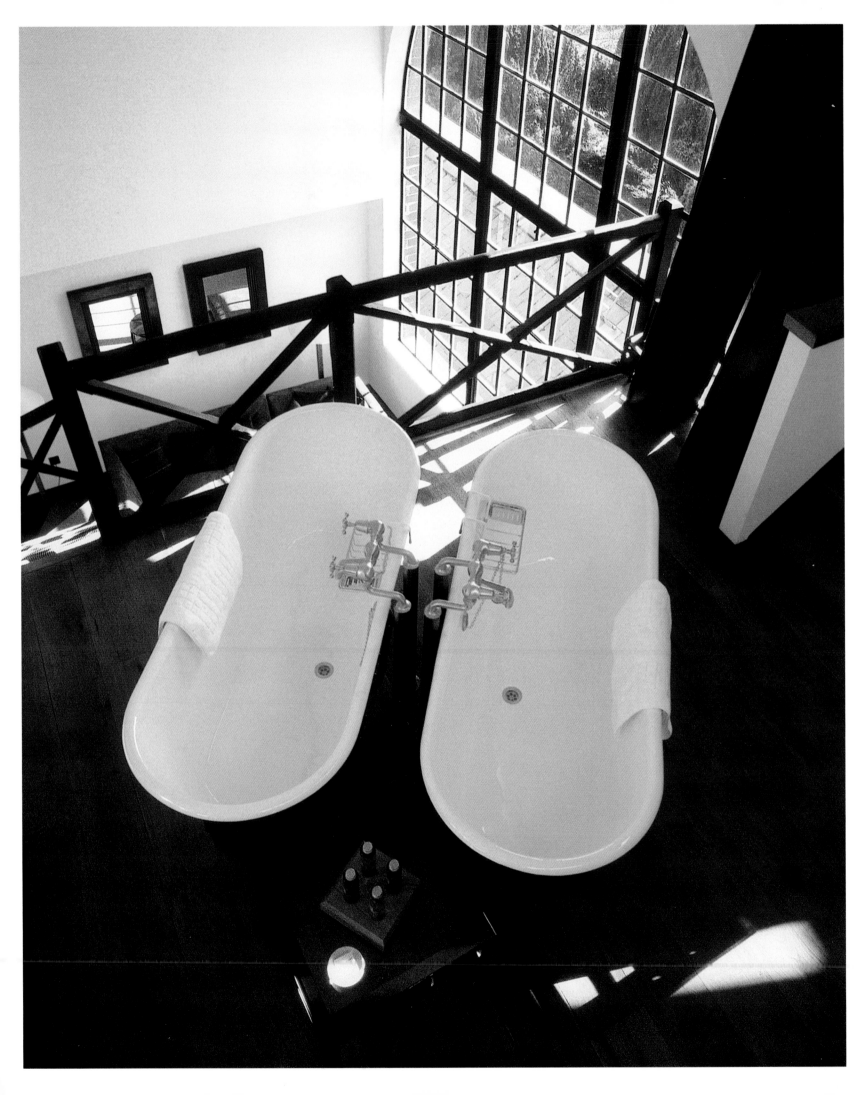

The building's past is apparent even in its refurbished state, due to the preservation of architectural features such as wooden beams, ironwork, and machinery from the old factory that is displayed in some of the rooms.

DAR LES CIGOGNES

This traditional Moroccan house, built during the seventeenth century, once belonged to a merchant who did business with the nearby royal palace of Marrakech. From thence came the storks that give their name to this hotel, which is the product of the labor of the architect Charles Boccara, the interior designer Tanja Tibaldi, and over 50 artists and craftspeople.

Although most of the original decorative features had already disappeared by the time the property was purchased, the structure was intact. The first phase of the project involved the refurbishing of the five-room house arranged about a patio and was completed in 2001. The second phase, which was finished three years later, involved the restoration of an adjoining edifice in which six additional rooms were made available, along with the Turkish bath and the shop. From the roof terraces of both buildings, which are joined by a bridge spanning a narrow street, magnificent vistas of the Atlas mountains can be enjoyed.

The motivation for the Les Cigognes project was to put on view Morocco's many-faceted, rich cultural and artistic heritage. Each room was individually designed, with traditional motifs, and named appropriately for the theme: Sahara, Berber, or Casablanca. The furniture and decorative items—among which the carved wooden doors, hammered silver mirrors, and bronze lamps are exceptional—are locally produced. The walls are finished throughout the hotel in *tadelakt,* a painstaking plasterwork that produces a shiny surface, while the floor is laid with handmade tiles or *das,* a substance similar to *tadelakt.* In the dining room, the Bordeaux *tadelakt* walls are ornamented with motifs from the Koran.

The simple doorway to Dar Les Cigognes conceals carefully designed interiors, arranged around patios where the sound of fountains and the aroma of citrus add to the charm of this establishment, which is characterized by luxurious but unostentatious accommodations.

Architect: **Charles Boccara**
Photography: **Dar Les Cigognes**
Opening date: **2004**
Number of rooms: **11**
Address: **108 rue de Berima Medina, Marrakech, Morocco**
Telephone: **+212 44 38 27 40**
Fax: **+212 44 38 47 67**
E-mail: **info@lescigognes.com**
Web site: **www.lescigognes.com**
Services: **restaurant, spa, Turkish bath, shop, roof terraces**

The hotel's 11 rooms were developed individually around themes taken from local culture. Left: The Berber Room, with Berber designs and decorative objects originating from this ancestral tribe. Top: The Safi Room is a tribute to the renowned Moroccan ceramics, of which several pieces are on display.

FCC ANGKOR

FCC Angkor is located in central Siem Reap, beside the river of the same name. The proximity of the fascinating Angkor Wat temples, world heritage since 1992, subtly distinguishes this GFAB project. However, instead of reproducing the esthetics of the temple complex itself, the architects sought to create an ambience similar to that of the temple experience by imitating the plan of small terraces set among ancient trees and pools with amazing reflections.

The project consisted of designing a large resort containing a wide variety of functional spaces—hotel, spa, galleries, restaurant, bar—each capable of operating independently but at the same time forming a coherent whole. During the first phase of construction, the former French consulate of Siem Reap, constructed during the 1950s, was extensively refurbished and extended to accommodate the bar and restaurant on the ground floor. A series of boutiques was located in the basement, which also allows access to the parking area. A long swimming pool connects the building with the outside area. The second phase of the project included building 29 rooms, two suites, and another swimming pool, as well as the spa and an additional shopping mall open to the street and overlooking the river.

One of the basic intentions in the design of FCC Angkor was to safeguard the magnificent trees that dominate the complex, so the buildings were adapted to allow room for the trees to flourish around them. Given the urban location, it was decided to erect the hotel with its back to the outside environment; thus, each room has a private balcony facing toward the interior patios. The linear architectural style of the new buildings is softened by the luxuriant vegetation and ever-changing reflections in the swimming pool, which is lined with black slate and designed to call to mind the lagoons adjoining the Angkor Wat temples.

Architects: **Gary Fell/GFAB Architects**
Photography: **Paul Stewart/Mouth to Source, Darren Campbell**
Opening date: **2004**
Number of rooms: **31**
Address: **Pokambor Avenue, Siem Reap, Cambodia**
Telephone: **+855 63 760 280**
Fax: **+855 63 760 281**
E-mail: **angkor@fcccambodia.com**
Web site: **www.fcccambodia.com**
Services: **bar, restaurant, spa, retail and art galleries, entertainment room, conference room, swimming pool**

Screened from the exterior by towering trees and aromatic gardens, an array of enclosed patios and swimming pools links the different buildings at the FCC Angkor.

The rooms, each one named for a Cambodian herb or spice, express the harmony and sophistication of GFAB Architects, responsible for the interior design and most of the furnishings.